MW00882373

ZEN

AND THE ART OF

CHRISTMAS LETTERS

BY CHUCK STORLA

NotQuiteProfitable Press

Printed in the United States of America
First Printing, 2017

www.chuckstorla.com

EARLY REVIEWS

"This is a book that I wish I could have written. It captures the spirit of Christmas much better than I managed." - Charles Dickens

"I envy the author's command of the English language." - Leo Tolstoy

"I know an epic when I see one, and this is certainly an epic." - Homer

"This is a super book." - Diana Prince, an Amazonian Book Review

"Lorem ipsum dolor sit amet, consectetur adipisicing elit, sed do eiusmod tempor incididunt ut labore et dolore magna aliqua." - Random Typesetter

"A rambling, stream-of-consciousness work that is part memoir, part self-help manual. The author's liberal use of footnotes may be a problem for some conservatives." - The Daily

Republican

"For years, I have been asking Chuck, 'how do you do it?' I have always meant to ask 'why do you do it?' Now, for better or worse, I know why." - Anonymous friend

"The book is so much better than the movie, or it would be if there was a movie." - @reallynotatroll

"#ZenandTheArtofChristmasLetters No matter how hard I try I am not able to do justice to this book in a measly one hundred and forty characte" - @reallynotatroll2

"Your relatives are already laughing at you. Make them get in line by laughing at yourself first." - Chuck Storla

"I found it to be a quick read and I've been moving kinda slow at the junction." - Uncle Joe

"A good book to take on a long plane trip." - Amelia E.

"What can I say? I loved it." - Chuck's Mother

DEDICATIONS

This book is dedicated to all the friends and relatives who claimed they loved my Christmas letters. As a result of your kind comments and gentle urging, I have written this book. Thank you for your encouragement over the years.

Now it is time for you to put up or shut up. Were you were being truthful when you said, "We love reading your letters. Please keep it up"? In that case, you should happily buy a copy of this book. In fact, you should buy several and give them as gifts. In particular, you should send a copy to the friends or family members who send you trite, boring or even painful Christmas letters each year.

This book is also dedicated to my children, Erik, Kari and Kristin, although they are hardly children at this point. I have used a part of your life story each year to add content to the Christmas letter. I often adjusted the truth to set up a punch line. Thank you for your understanding. Just think how much worse it would be if I posted this on Facebook and tagged you so your friends could read it. If that doesn't make you feel better then just suck it up. Consider it part of a tough-love parenting scheme. Better late than never.

Finally, I dedicate this book to my wife, Karin, who suffered in silence (for the most part) as I procrastinated each year. My routine was to produce a Christmas letter days, or at times hours, before Christmas. I often left her no chance to get the letters stuffed into our Christmas cards with any hope of them arriving on time. In this, as in many things, I am truly sorry.

I will no doubt do it again this year.

FOREWORD

Tradition will tell you that a respected person or well-known figure writes the Foreword of a book. This individual can bring some of their credibility to the task. Their job is to convince the reader that this new book by an unknown author is really worth reading. Unfortunately, I do not know any respected people, much less any who are well known. Thus the task fell back on me. I am not respected, but at least I know me.

I could have left off the foreword entirely, but I needed the word count. This seemed like an easy place to get a few more sentences while at the same time not worrying too much about the content. After all, no one ever reads the Foreward of a book. If by any chance you happen to be reading this I advise you to just jump directly to the Preface.

PREFACE

Why *Zen and the Art of Christmas Letters*, you ask? According to the Ultimate Source of Knowledge[1], Zen "de-emphasizes mere knowledge ... and favors direct understanding through ... interaction with an **accomplished teacher**."

The de-emphasis of mere knowledge is consistent with current trends in our culture. Facebook and Twitter allow one to not only de-emphasize knowledge but ignore it altogether. We have a cable channel claiming to be "The History Channel" that includes programming on ancient astronauts, Nostradamus and the paranormal. Knowledge is unnecessary when one can blindly leap to direct understanding.

The Wikipedia excerpt given above also demonstrates one method we can use to facilitate our blind leaps. There is great power, without the accompanying responsibility, in taking an arbitrary excerpt and then replacing sections with ellipses.[2] This can be done without regard for the missing sections and the resulting missing content. It is a handy device when you want to change the meaning to fit your own agenda. Several news websites have raised this practice to an art form.

This is all to say that I realize that I have combined a random set of associations with an unrelated Asian philosophy. Nothing more is required to bridge the gulf between Zen and the practice of writing a Christmas letter.

禅 = Zen

+

圣诞信 = Christmas letter

In the spirit of full disclosure, I should also mention that I felt this title was evocative of the excellent and completely unrelated, *Zen and the Art of Motorcycle Maintenance*. The title I chose was also more marketable than the working title, *How to Write a Christmas Letter That Doesn't Suck*.

Furthermore, in the same spirit, I should mention that there is little, if any, reference to Zen or any other Asian philosophy in the rest of this book. Like I said, it fixed a problem with the title.

Dear reader, I hope that you will read this book in its entirety even though I have revealed its narrow and arbitrary foundation. I want to be your **accomplished teacher**.[3]

As your **accomplished teacher**, I promise to lead you to a deeper understanding of the Christmas letter in ritual and practice. At the end of this book, you may find that you have a better understanding of yourself, your desires and your place in the universe. Then again, you might not.

Chuck Storla, July 2017
Somewhere on Earth, but
Not the North Pole

[1] The Ultimate Source of Knowledge, aka Wikipedia, was used to provide the quotation which was then manipulated for my purpose.
[2] According to Vocabulary.com, "An ellipsis is punctuation that is used to show where words have been left out." Perhaps a better definition is to simply say, "it is the dot, dot, dot."
[3] I am intentionally putting this in bold type so

that when you see it later in the book you will remember our respective roles. My hope is that it keeps you from challenging my authority.

How to read this book.

WORD ORDER
Read the words from left to right. Begin at the top and proceed to the bottom of each page before moving to the next.

FOOTNOTES
Pay attention to the footnotes or you will miss some significant bits of knowledge and a chance to win big money![1]

---

[1] The part about winning money is a lie, but this was good practice for you in reading footnotes.

CONTENTS

Chapters

Table of Contents

ZEN AND THE ART OF
CHRISTMAS LETTERS

I

The State of the Art

I believe that Christmas letters are the fruitcakes of the literary world. At least once in life, everyone sends one, but no one likes to receive one.

Here are the facts:[1] Most Christmas letters are as boring to write, as they are to read. They tend to be a chronology of your family's last year. If you remember correctly, it was not that much fun to live through the first time. Now you are forced to relive each disappointment and near miss. You recount all the milestones you stumbled over and the millstones that fell on top of you. This is never a pleasant experience for you as a writer, and I for one do not want to read about it.

As the author of a Christmas letter, your readers fall into one of two camps. The first group knows you well. They are already aware of the mess your life has been over the last twelve months. The other group does not know you well. For these people, they are unaware of your personal hardships. In all probability, they do not care in the least. So it is either redundant or unnecessary for you to send a Christmas letter to either group. Whether you were aware of this or not, you have continued to produce a letter each year and inflict it on your friends and family.

My objective in this book is to guide you to a fresh approach for your Christmas letter. Insanity is defined as doing the same thing over and over while expecting a different result. This means that sanity must be trying something new and not caring about the result.

If you follow the advice I provide, you will leave insanity behind and become the sanest member of your family. If your family is anything like mine, I suspect the bar is not that high. Still, it is something to shoot for.

[1] To be more accurate I should have said, "Here

18

is the fact," but that just doesn't have the same impact.

II

My Journey

To be honest, I have known for a number of years that no one was reading my Christmas letters. That did nothing to stop me. Like many of you, I simply fell into the habit of writing an annual letter. I described life as experienced in our household - the comings and goings, the ups and downs and the mostly sideways. My wife and I added a few cute pictures of our kids. They were still cute at the time even without Photoshop. Then we tucked a letter into each card we mailed out of state. We did not include a Christmas letter in the cards we sent locally[1] for reasons that will be obvious later.

From the very first year I mailed out our family Christmas letter, I heard back comments such as,

"We loved reading your letter."

"We really enjoyed hearing about Aaron and Deanne."

"Your letter was the best one we received this year."

I should have caught on right then. These were the exact same lies that I had been telling our friends and family members about their Christmas letters. It also seemed strange that they left out one of our kids and called the other two wrong names.

It was not until a few years later that the truth hit me like a keyboard in the forehead; literally like a keyboard in the forehead. I had just finished writing what I thought would be the best Christmas letter I had ever written. I began to proofread the first draft, and noticed that I had typed "jmu lojufr" several times in just the first page.

I had no idea how this strange text got into my letter, so I did what any normal person would do. I rebooted Windows. I ran several antivirus programs. I reinstalled my word processor.

None of this seemed to solve the problem or reveal the underlying cause. In spite of graduating from a liberal arts college, I had a good understanding of The Scientific Method. I created a hypothesis and set out to test it through experimentation. My hypothesis was that I had somehow overcome my Lutheran upbringing. The garbled text was a result of speaking or, more accurately, typing in tongues. Creating an experiment to test this hypothesis was more difficult than I expected.

Like many great discoveries, this was when serendipity tripped over happenstance, bounced off random occurrence and slammed into blind chance. I was frustrated and began to hit my head against the keyboard. There, in front of me on the screen, was exactly the character string from the Christmas letter. It was not produced as a result of any metaphysical transmission. The characters were produced when my forehead hit the keyboard and then rolled to the left. It occurred several times almost letter for letter. This demonstrated several things. First of all, I must have been very consistent in dropping my head onto the center of the keyboard as I fell asleep. Second, the left side of my head was apparently heavier than the right.[2]

As an experiment, I printed that letter and
mailed it to my friends and family, complete
with every "jmu   lojufr" intact. In response, I
received precisely nothing. Silence. An empty
mailbox. I thought at least one of my aunts
would suspect an embedded satanic message,
and call for an exorcism.[3] I was not prepared for
this silence so I called several of the people on
my out-of-state mailing list and casually asked,
"How did you like our Christmas letter this
year?"

Every response was some variation on:
>"We loved reading your letter."
>"We really enjoyed hearing about
>Aaron and Deanne."
>"Your letter was the best one we
>received this year."

My first guess was that each of these randomly
selected friends and family members just
happened to be accomplished liars. Then I
remembered that several of them did not
possess that skill, nor any other. The only
conclusion I could reach was that while reading

my letter they had all fallen asleep before they even got to the point of trying to decide what to make of "jmu lojufr."

The following year I took my testing to a new level. I simply took the previous year's letter and sent it to the same list. I did not even bother to change the date at the top, nor did I put in any new pictures. The result was the same. At first, I heard nothing, and then came the inevitable:

"We loved reading your letter."

"We really enjoyed hearing about Aaron and Deanne."

"Your letter was the best one we received this year."

Once again I surmised that all of my readers had succumbed to sleep before they finished the first paragraph. Upon waking I am sure they simply went on to the next Christmas letter in their pile without another thought given to mine.

Certain by now that I had stumbled on a trend, I searched for the stack of Christmas letters that we had received that year. I found them propping up a slightly too-short table leg.

Reading through the letters one by one, I found multiple patterns similar to the following: "jmuIk,,,,,,,,,iolp;[']"

Extrapolating from my previous results, I was able to determine that my friends and family were almost exclusively dropping their foreheads on their keyboards but then rolling to the right. This was clear evidence that these individuals right-brain-heavy.[4] It also implied they were as bored writing their letters as I was writing mine.

Using my collection of family and friends as a representative sample[5] of the entire country, I realized that when each of us wrote and distributed our Christmas letters we were not just boring the recipients. We were going above and beyond. We were boring ourselves even as we wrote them. At that pivotal moment, I determined that I was going to challenge this sad state of affairs as soon as I was done pivoting. It was beginning to make me dizzy anyway. I was tired of reading and writing boring Christmas letters. I was also running out of excuses at work to explain why it appeared that I had slept through the night with my face planted on a keyboard.

Using the techniques that I will share with you in this book, I turned things around and started to produce Christmas letters that people enjoyed reading. Even more importantly, I started to produce Christmas letters that I had fun writing.

Since changing my ways and learning to write Christmas letters that do not put people to sleep, I have been receiving scores of comments like these:

> "We loved reading your letter. No, really, this time we mean it."
>
> "We enjoyed hearing about Erik, Kari, and Kristin."
>
> "When are you going to send us your Christmas letter? We look forward to it every year."

Chances are good that two out of three are sincere and they finally got the right names for our kids.

I want you to be able to share in this experience. You can do it. Your Christmas letters can be fun for both you and your readers. What do you have to lose other than the imprint of the keyboard on your forehead?[6]

[1] If you are a friend living near us and have never received one of our award-winning Christmas letters, you will find copies on sale in the lobby at the close of our show.

[2] Some might say this is due to a prominent and predominantly empty area on the right side of my brain. I prefer to assume it is due to a massive cluster of super brain cells on the left. It may not be science, but it is my delusion so let me have it.

[3] That is an exaggeration. We Lutherans are not big on the idea of exorcisms since it requires a tremendous amount of energy and unrestrained demonstration of emotions. It is OK for others, but it is just not something we are comfortable with. We will learn to live with any demon provided it keeps a low profile and the neighbors do not notice.

[4] I was not sure how I felt being the only logical person in a group of right-brained creative types, but science does not lie. Science is fully capable of misleading, teasing, taunting and baiting, but it never lies outright.

[5] My family and friends may not be entirely representative of the entire country. My sample is biased as it a) is predominantly midwestern, b) includes a disproportionate number of Scandinavians, and c) contains a non-trivial number of geeks/nerds and people that can never quite match the items in their wardrobe since they outgrew their Garanimals.

[6] If you are suffering from morning keyboard-face, consider getting one of the new MacBooks. Their keyboards, like my writing, leave much less of an impression.

III

THE QUESTION

Philosophers will tell you that some of the great questions of humanity are "What is the meaning of life?", "What is reality?", and "Do we have free will?" Men and women with great minds have spent decades pondering these questions. While I do not have the intellect or the credentials of the great thinkers, I can tell you without a doubt they missed the most fundamental philosophical question. The central question is one that applies to any task, large or small. This is true whether the task is seeking a basic understanding of the universe or something really important like writing a Christmas letter. That question is:

Why bother?[1]

Given that I raised the question, I will now try to answer it. You will note throughout this book that I tend not to raise any questions that I cannot at least pretend to answer.[2]

This book is ostensibly non-fiction, which is not to claim that it is true. However, I will insert some pseudo-scientific rationale to bolster an otherwise flimsy premise. See if you can follow along.

Inanimate objects move only when an external agent causes them to move. Consider the age-old statement, "These dishes are not going to wash themselves." In this instance, the dishes are inanimate objects which are unable to move on their own or wash themselves. On the other hand, living things are able to move of their own volition or when prompted by a spouse with even more volition.

To understand this distinction, consider an instance in which my father-in-law is watching sports on a Sunday afternoon. My mother-in-law would verbalize a variation of the "not going to wash themselves" statement. The end result would be that my father-in-law would move to the kitchen of his own volition if he knew what was good for him.

To continue the thought experiment, consider what would happen if an impartial observer were to ask my father-in-law why he was washing the dishes (i.e., "Why bother?"). My father-in-law's first response would probably be along the lines of "Who the hell are you and why are you in my house?" He might then begin to look around with suspicion and ask, "Is this another of my damn son-in-law's thought experiments?" We can now see that there are things that sound fine in a Philosophy 101 classroom that do not work within the confines of my family.

Leaving my father-in-law as he lets the water out of the sink and begins to dry, we will return to the distinction between inanimate objects and living things. Human beings are the most advanced among all living things. To some, this means that human beings are the crown of creation. Alternatively, others would describe human beings as the party hat of creation. Either way, as the crown/party hat of creation, we have free will. We roll downhill, not merely as a result of gravity, but often from doing something stupid, ingesting something stupid, or both. We move of our own volition. Often we move to get farther from those who annoy us. This may explain the empty space around you at this moment.

Human beings also have intelligence. At least I do. The jury is still out with regard to you. In fact, the jury went out for their lunch break and have not been seen or heard from since. I guess you should be grateful that I showed up and can do the thinking for the two of us.

Back to the crown/party hat analogy (which we should now realize represents me and you, respectively). Let us remain under the assumption that we have intelligence, and that we can make free and independent choices. The most fundamental of these choices is whether to bother at all. You will be forgiven if you lost track, but this brings us to the point of this chapter: why should we bother to write Christmas letters?

To answer this question, we first need to look at the underlying purpose of an annual Christmas letter. Why would any individual John Doe write a Christmas letter? On the surface, it might appear that his purpose would be to give friends and relatives an update on the Doe family. That is an illusion. The real purpose of a Christmas letter is for the Doe family to convince their friends, family, and enemies (often overlapping sets of people) that life in the Doe family is wonderful. In fact, life in the Doe family is much better than the pitiful existence that the friends, family, and enemies are experiencing.

The goal of a Christmas letter is not to inform but rather to create intense feelings of envy, if not self-loathing, on the part of the reader. That is because in the harsh light of reality the letter writer's life is not that great. At least not great enough to impress your brother-in-law who barely made it out of high school, but now is the sole owner of a profitable chain of 15-minute oil change shops.

Since the Christmas letter is not written to inform, we can dispense with archaic concepts such as facts, the objective truth or any connection to reality. Any attempt to bring in facts/truth/reality doomed to failure. It is sure to produce a boring Christmas letter. It will also fail to induce appropriate levels of envy in your brother-in-law.

At the same time, you do not want to get caught with obvious, or at least easily discoverable, falsehoods. This means that your Christmas letter departures from reality need to be written in such a manner that your reader will never uncover the underlying "truth." If needed we can always fall back on the standard used by at least one three-letter television news organization - "even if the documents are false, the underlying story is true."

For another example we can learn from, the CIA has worked for years to perfect the concept of "plausible deniability." Their only mistake in the recent decade was keeping copies of too many emails. We can all learn from that. While it remains to be seen if this is a good or bad idea, the CIA has a Facebook page. That seems strange for an allegedly covert organization. I mention this only so I can segue into the next paragraph.

Speaking of Facebook, there are some helpful lessons that we can glean from looking at how people use Facebook. These lessons can be applied directly to our Christmas letters. Both Facebook and a Christmas letter are used for a similar purpose: to lie to our friends and family about how wonderful our life is.

The end goal is to convince our readers that by comparison, their family is a bunch of underachievers. They never go anywhere near as cool as we do. They do not eat at the great restaurants where we regularly dine. Unlike us, they do not accomplish anything noteworthy. Finally, and perhaps most important, they could not produce a good quality selfie if their social life depended on it; which apparently it does.

How do you create this illusion of a perfect family existence? Just think of your life from the perspective of a politician or soft drink's ad agency. You need to generate a perception that is strong enough to overcome any real-life evidence to the contrary. If you do this properly you may begin to believe it yourself. For example, consider what can happen if your Christmas letter implies (never state anything outright) that your son is running a highly profitable hedge fund. When your aunt runs into your son on the street, she should be so bought into that image that she can look beyond the scraggly hair, torn t-shirt, and dirty cutoffs. She will simply assume that he has so much wealth and power that he does not need to impress anyone with his outward appearance. She will see him as a successful tycoon-in-the-making. In turn, she will feel somewhat ashamed of her own son, the lowly bank vice president. She had been proud of him until she learned that his title simply meant he manages three tellers and monitors the drive-through ATM at the local branch.

While this was simply an example, I should point out that you need to consider your current circumstances and your audience. Depending on the ratio of red to blue in your family and friends base, you may want to modify your son's fictional hedge fund to one focused on environmentally friendly companies. On the other hand, if you intend to hit up family members for a loan in the next month, you may want to hint that your son is working for an inner-city non-profit rather than a hedge fund.

In the end (at least the end of this chapter), we come back to the question, "Why bother?" We have seen that a Christmas letter can be used to simultaneously impress and depress the recipients. In later chapters, we will see how it can be entertaining for the writer and possibly entertaining for the reader as well. Perhaps a complete answer to "Why bother?", is that a well-conceived Christmas letter can hit all the levels of Maslow's Hierarchy of Needs. That is a grand enough concept to require its own chapter.

[1] The more astute among you have probably been asking yourselves that question for some time now.

[2] I learned this lesson from watching the prosecuting attorneys on "Law & Order". If you ignore this lesson, things will not end well. The exception occurs when the question-without-a-known-answer is asked at the forty-five minute mark. This still allows the issue to get resolved in nine minutes (allowing for commercials).

IV

MASLOW'S HIERARCHY

Anyone who was fortunate enough to sit
through a semester of social "science" and mind
games (otherwise known as Psychology 101) has
encountered Maslow's Hierarchy of Needs. If
you managed to dodge that cerebral bullet then
you may have run into the famous pyramid
when it was used by a motivational speaker or
sales trainer. It is one of those theoretical
constructs that can be molded into more shapes
than Play-Doh.[1] It lends a veneer of academic
respectability to a presentation in the same way
that a token "real" journalist can lend a veneer
of objectivity to an otherwise partisan news
organization.

For those who have never heard of Maslow's
Hierarchy, or long forgotten what they knew of

it, the following graphic shows the most common version.

Self-Actualization

Esteem

Love/ Belonging

Safety

Physiological

At first glance, we can see the obvious similarity between Maslow's pyramid and a Christmas tree. Many reputable conspiracy theories have been built on little more than this. This allows me to be comfortable claiming a solid link between Maslow's theories and Christmas letters. This represents not one but a minimum of two layers of academic veneer and will soon approach IKEA levels of coverage.

PHYSIOLOGICAL

Starting at the bottom, we have the "physical requirements for human survival". A Christmas letter doesn't have anything to offer here unless you find yourself alone in the woods with plenty of logs but no tinder to start a fire. In that case, a stack of Christmas letters could be rolled up and used to get the fire going. I am sure some of my early letters were used in just this way. I realize this is a stretch but hang in there. The good stuff is coming up.

SAFETY

OK. So we are not to the good stuff yet. Other than paper cuts, there are not too many dangers associated with Christmas letters. That said, remember to wear your seatbelt and be sure to wash your hands after handling raw chicken. Next.

LOVE/BELONGING

Now we are getting to the heart of the matter. Done correctly, a Christmas letter is the epitome of self-love. It can give you a feeling of belonging to a better social level than you actually inhabit. According to the Ultimate Source of Knowledge, "the third level of human needs is interpersonal and involves feelings of belongingness." A word of friendly advice here from your **accomplished teacher.**[2] Never use the word "belongingness" at a party. You will find yourself suddenly surrounded by ten feet of empty personal space.[3] It is probably a good idea to avoid it in any circumstance, which makes me wonder why I did not heed my own advice.

ESTEEM

This is where the meat of a Christmas letter shines, or it would if meat could shine. Maslow described two versions of esteem: getting the respect of others and having self-esteem. A well-crafted Christmas letter will earn not just the respect of others, but if you are lucky, their envy. Should you manage to believe your own fabricated narratives, then your self-esteem will improve as well. If not, then get some comfort from knowing you lowered it for others.

SELF-ACTUALIZATION

We must start this section with a warning. You should only use this term when safely within the bounds of this book. Do not attempt any other use on your own. [4]

"What a man can be, he must be." - Abraham Maslow

I appreciate the zen-like nature of this brief sentence as it struggles to become a tautology.

To some, this is evidence of the theory's underlying genius. While to others it is evidence of the theory's underlying misogyny.

The US Army attempted to use this need as a recruitment pitch in saying to us, "Be All You Can Be." Motivational speakers have linked the fulfillment of this need to using their "proven" techniques for day-trading, flipping real estate or selling household products to neighbors. To some, reaching self-actualization is only achieved by exceeding their monthly sales quota. If he was aware of these developments, this might explain why Maslow saw the need for yet a higher level.

SELF-TRANSCENDENCE
This one never made it to the many PowerPoint slides with multi-layer pyramids for obvious reasons. In fact, it did not make it to the graphic[5] earlier in this chapter. No one understands what Dr. Maslow meant by it. Experience has shown that Self-transcendence is only relevant when people are experiencing an altered state, such as California.

SUMMARY
I have tried to create a solid connection[6]

between the Christmas letter and Maslow's Hierarchy of Needs. If I succeeded then I have applied a nice layer of respectability and academic veneer to the top of my pressed wood concoction of recycled concepts and particulate matter. As you proceed through the rest of this book, be careful of the edges.

[1] When molding Maslow's Hierarchy to fit into your own theories, be sure to use the name brand version. The homemade play dough often gets moldy when exposed to the air for too long.

[2] Refer back to the Preface if you do not remember who this is.

[3] The exception to this advice occurs when you want to get ten feet of empty personal space. In that case, this is a proven method. I have found it invaluable in certain situations.

[4] To be absolutely certain you remain unharmed, the term "self-actualization" should only be used in public when you are in a "safe space." This is likely to be found on a liberal arts campus.

[5] Made you look, didn't I?

[6] I have no doubt that within a few years someone with a larger vocabulary and greater capacity for BS will turn this chapter into a

successful doctoral dissertation. It has happened
before.

V

Your Toolbox

Prior to the start of any project, a wise person should assemble the correct tools. As you have probably assumed by now, I chose to jump in feet first and think of things like life preservers only after I start sinking. I find that as I begin to submerge, I achieve a clarity of mind just prior to the thrashing and screaming. During this brief time of clarity, I have insights into what I should have done to prepare. Thanks to my years of experimentation, I have assembled a list of items that will help you along the way.

Gather the following materials prior to starting on your Christmas letter:

1) Book
2) ADD

3) Computer
4) Paper
5) Printer
6) Ink
7) Family photographs
8) Adult beverage

In the following paragraphs, I will expand on the need for each item and its proper use.

1) A book will come in handy. At least it will if is **this book**. By now you should have learned how much you are in need of its advice as you prepare to write the best Christmas letter of your life. Congratulations on having the wisdom to obtain a copy. If you would like to write an even better letter in half the time, you could purchase a second copy.

2) **ADD** stands for Attention Deficit Disorder. In writing your letter, it helps to have on hand a good case of ADD or, at a minimum, a six-pack. At my house, we have it on draft. ADD is very helpful to keep you from falling into the trap of linear and logical thinking.

If you do not already have ADD, you might consider hanging out at a middle school, where you stand a good chance of catching it. Bear in mind that if you do not have a child who is a student at that middle school, you may need to budget for legal fees as well.

Note that Hyperactivity is strictly optional.

3) A **computer** - preferably one from HP. I own a few shares of their stock and the share price could use a boost.

If you are a closet Luddite, you can go really old school and use a typewriter or even pen each letter by hand. For a really unique twist on the Christmas letter tradition, you can cut individual letters from magazines and newspapers. When you arrange these letters and paste them to paper, it gives the appearance of a ransom note. While this demonstrates your unique personality, you may also need to budget some legal fees for this one.

4) A ream or two of **paper**. Any color will do as long as it is a light color. You may have been Goth when you were in high school, but black printing on black paper does not work well. Traditionalists may also consider it inappropriate for a Christmas letter.

5) A **printer** - preferably an HP (see above).

6) Lots of HP-branded **ink** for your printer. (Also see above)

There is one instance where you may want to consider using refillable ink cartridges. Let's assume there is content in your Christmas letter that you do not want to follow you for the rest of your life. Use the cheapest ink possible. Then recommend that your recipients leave the letter face-up in the sun. That way you are guaranteed that in a year the ink will have faded away. You will no longer risk being caught in an obvious fabrication. As much fun as it is to fabricate things, you do not want to cause yourself problems in a future court case or family reunion.[1]

7) A collection of **photographs** of your family or photographs of the people that you would like to see in your family (more on this in a later chapter).

8) The **adult beverage** is a necessity. I will leave you to decide if you use it in preparation for writing or in celebration of completion.

[1] I hope these are not one and the same events for you and yours.

VI

WHY BE FUNNY?

After "Why bother?", the second most fundamental Christmas letter question is "Why be funny?" The simple answer is that it is more fun to be funny and less fun to not be funny.

I am certain that somewhere back in time, the words "fun" and "funny" come from the same Latin root. I do not know since I never took Latin and did badly in the two years of French I attempted. Re-reading the first sentence of this chapter, I can guess that "fundamental" comes from the same root as "fun." Somehow I doubt that, but it could be true. Maybe I should have taken Latin in place of French. I might have done better, but then the girls in the French class were cuter. Get out any high school yearbook. Look at the pictures of the Latin club and then the French club. Now, do you understand what I mean?

There is a second reason to be funny. When you take a light-hearted approach to your Christmas letter, then your reader will as well. They will be less critical and assume that the clumsy gaffe in the middle of the first paragraph was not a mistake but a clever attempt at humor. If you set the tone properly, they will even find humor in things you did not intend to be funny. No one wants to be the one who does not get the joke. Your readers will assume they are missing something and chuckle along even when they are clueless.[1]

Even if you cannot make your Christmas letter fun to read at least make it fun to write. No one wants to read a boring letter and you really do not want to be bored while writing one. Personally, I toil and sweat over each Christmas letter I write for at least thirty minutes. There have been times when I have spent up to an hour writing one if the TV is on. Why put up with being bored for that long a stretch when you can have fun with it?

I do not know you, but I think I know

something about you. You see some, if not all, of the universe is revolving around you right now. Consider how you drive in rush-hour traffic. I am right, aren't I? In your eyes, you are possibly the most important person in the universe. It is only your world-class humility that prevents you from pointing it out to others. Given that you are this important, why should you have to be bored writing a Christmas letter? You owe it to yourself to have fun with it.

How do you make it fun? As you would expect from your **accomplished teacher**, I have a few suggestions.

1) Don't take yourself too seriously. Trust me, no one else does.

2) Place little land mines in your letter that you know will delight, upset or confound specific family members. An oblique reference to a family member's old girlfriend or boyfriend is one possibility.

3) Include pop culture references or Internet memes that only the teenagers in the house will understand. Even if you are not there to see it, it is priceless when your nieces and nephews are laughing at their parents' expense.

4) Be sure to include at least one word that will force people to search for a dictionary or other reference work. This one is not only fun but reinforces that you are smarter than they are. At a minimum, it demonstrates that you have a thesaurus and aren't afraid to use it.

5) Be sure to liberally[2] use self-deprecating humor. Unless you live in a red state and then you will have to conservatively use self-deprecating humor.

Getting back to your place of comfort, let us revisit you-as-the-center-of-everything. As mentioned above, if it isn't fun for them to read, at least make it fun for you to write. If you are uncomfortable with this level of self-interest then consider the alternative. If you make your reader the center-of-everything, then you are just feeding their narcissistic tendencies. They are perfectly capable of doing that themselves. They do not need your help in this and may come to resent you for it.

Finally, if your readers are so sour that they cannot find any humor in your letter, then just remember the famous Latin phrase, "Skrūvju tos, ja viņi nevar veikt joks." [3]

[1] It is a demonstrated fact that 87% of everyone's relatives are clueless. As a field test, attend your next family reunion. You will find ample evidence to support this statistic. Before you get too arrogant, remember that you are also someone's relative. That individual is considering the same statistic at this very moment and looking your way.

[2] You likely did not recall that there is a similar bit of word play on liberal/liberally in the "Early Reviews". This is an example of how you can rely on your reader's limited short-term memory. Feel free to reuse a joke multiple times in the same letter. If a reader does happen to call you on it just tell them that it is a running joke. That should quiet them for a bit as they try to figure it out.

[3] This translates as "Screw them if they cannot take a joke." I realize that this sounds harsh in English which is why I first offered it in Latin. Anything said in Latin takes on the weight of history and benefits from an assumption that it was taken from an academic paper.

[Addendum to the footnote]
My apologies. This was an error in the initial copy that somehow was not caught when we

went to press. This is not the Latin translation but the Latvian translation. My bad.

VII

YOUR AUDIENCE

Now that you have been [enlightened, manipulated, shamed - choose one] into writing a humorous letter, you need to consider your audience. This is something that I failed to do in writing this book. Unfortunately, I am in too deep to change now. We will both have to live with the consequences.

You may be tempted to skip over this chapter because you think you already know everything there is to know about your audience. Yes, obviously the audience for a Christmas letter is your friends and family. We still need to consider how to divide this large group into more manageable pieces.

We start by breaking your audience into two

groups. Just to keep things entertaining, these two groups will not be the same two groups mentioned in the first chapter. In this chapter, the first group is the people who like you and the second group contains the people who do not like you. Notice I did not say that these are two halves. Chances are real good that the audience is heavily weighted in favor of those who do not like you. The longer you have been sending Christmas letters, the more haters there will be.

Let us start with the first subgroup - all of those people who only wish the best for you and think the best of you. Realistically, this group consists of just your mother. Add your father if you are currently on his good side. How long has it been since you put that dent in his new car? How reliable is his memory these days?

The people in the second group include those who are jealous of you or just feel inadequate when they see others being happier and more successful. This is basically everyone other than your mother and possibly your father.

The people who like you
The good news is that writing for the first group

is very simple. In my case, my mother loved everything I did. At least she loved the things I was willing to let her read. My mother was just happy that I wrote a letter and sent her a copy. The content was never important and I don't think she cared that it went to eighty other people. Every letter she received from me was special.

Fortunately for me, my mother was raised in the Midwest in an age when sarcasm had not yet penetrated to the center of the country.[1] The closest thing they had to a smart ass was a smart aleck. While both titles no doubt come from the same Latin roots, an aleck is still operating within the bounds of civility and good taste. Somewhere in my teens, I stepped across that boundary and have not looked back. Fortunately, I was successful in keeping this a secret from my mother. As a result, there were parts of my letters that she found funny and other parts that she did not quite understand.

This demonstrates one of the first things to consider when writing for the audience that likes you - never say anything mean or hurtful unless you are confident that they won't catch on. In other words, do not say anything in direct language when a simple obfuscation will let you get away with saying what you mean. For example, you should never refer to someone as an idiot. The better alternative is to link him or her to a novel by Dostoyevsky. This falls nicely under suggestions #2 (land mines) and #4 (requiring the use of reference works) from the last chapter.

I am sure that some of you think this is a bit severe. You do not think that a Christmas letter is any place for insults. I agree with you completely. I would never stoop to insulting anyone who would recognize they are being insulted. I am sure you, dear reader, do not feel that you have been insulted in the previous chapters. See how that works?

Having established that we can say anything we want to the people who love us and who see only the good, let's move on. We need to consider those who do not really care for us as individuals or who have not liked any of our letters up to this point.

The people who do not like you
The first thing you need to ask yourself is why do you care what these people think? Have you

asked yourself that question? Good. I bet I can tell you how you answered it. You do not care what they think. If you answered it any other way, it is time to get over high school.

Now that we have that understanding, we can focus on the third group of the two groups we started with. I possibly should have told you at the beginning of this chapter that there were more than two groups. I was not sure you could handle it at the time. Since then you have proven yourself capable of great things. I am sure you are ready now.

All the rest

This third group is by far the largest. They land somewhere between the unfailing love of a mother and the undying hatred of a rival. These are the brother/sister/aunt/uncle/niece/nephew/first cousin/second cousin twice removed/in-law/once-twice-three-times-a-lady/high school friends/college acquaintances and others who over the years have managed to find their way on to your Christmas card list. These are the people who, while not perfect, are at least worth a card and a 49¢ stamp. I realize it is a pretty low bar, but you would be surprised how many people you know who do not even make this cut. Back when stamps were 24¢ they were on the list but at today's rate, no way.

So this third group is the primary audience for your Christmas letter. These are the people that through accident of birth, accident of marriage,[2] or random acquaintance are on "The List". We must also add the people who, for no discernible reason, continue to mail us Christmas cards long after we have forgotten how we even know them.

For lack of a better title, let's give the people on the list the title of "the forty-nine-cent-ers".[3] In my original outline, this chapter was the place where I planned to break down this audience in great detail. The goal was a detailed dissection of the forty-nine-cent-ers so that we could understand them as well as you understand anyone. I planned to show you what characteristics they shared so that you could sculpt your letter to their common interests. I gave it an honest try, but it turned into a serious amount of work. On top of that, your second cousin in Iowa does not have much overlap with your spouse's great aunt in Seattle. Neither of them has the worldview of your freshman roommate with a strange address who sends envelopes that always appear to have been opened and then resealed.

Since I decided to avoid that serious amount of work, let me continue by stating generalities as if they were proven facts. At first glance, that shortcut may seem dangerous. I had hoped by this point you would blindly accept everything I said. However, if you do have any lingering doubts about me as your **accomplished teacher**, go to the item in the appendices with the title "Why Trust Me?" Go ahead and read it now. I'll be right here when you get back. Just put your finger on this spot so you know where to come back to.

I am glad we got that out of the way so that we can now proceed with our discussion of your audience.

Given that your friends and family are extremely common, you would expect for them to have some commonality. It turns out they don't. In fact, the only thing they share in common is you. This means you will not only be the writer of your Christmas letter, but you need to be a stand-in for your audience as well. You are the forty-nine-cent-er of all forty-nine-cent-ers. In pursuit of knowledge of your audience, we are forced to ask - who are you?

I think it is pretty clear that you are someone of average intelligence. If you were at the top of the intelligence continuum, you would have become bored with this book by now. The Dostoyevsky reference earlier would have triggered a memory and you would be off to your bookshelf to reread *The Brothers Karamazov*. Following that, you would have sat down to make a correction to the novel's Wikipedia article before moving on to the next shiny object that caught your intellectual interest. I would not expect to see "intellectual you" here again, so that must not be you. Sorry. The fact that you arrived at this point pretty much eliminates the possibility that you are a genius. I suspect you knew that.

You are part of the lump in the normal curve. Pat yourself on the back. Congratulations or condolences depending on your previous self-image. Now proceed with the conviction that you are the best example of your intended audience that exists. At least you are the best example of your intended audience within easy reach. In addition, using yourself as a stand-in for your readers means that at least one of your audience members will get every joke.

Unique members of your audience

While most average audience members are by definition average, there may be certain people on your Christmas list who require a different approach. I am speaking, of course, of a rich relative who is in ill health. This individual will require special treatment. I suggest that for them you drop the Christmas letter entirely. You do not want to risk them finding anything in your letter that will adversely affect the reading of the will.

A Worthy Heir

If you would like to convey your capacity to carry on the family name and some of the family fortune, then go out and buy a special Christmas card. Skip the dollar store and get something embossed that fits your relative's religious beliefs and worldview. Then include a family picture that will make them proud to consider you an heir. Buy a stock photo or use Photoshop as needed.[4]

Impoverished But Still Worthy

On the other hand, this might be a time when it would be wiser to demonstrate need over worthiness. In that case, go directly to the dollar store for the appropriate card. While still at the store, drive over the card you bought once or twice in the parking lot. When you get home, make sure it looks like the entire Cratchit family signed it. For good measure, include one of Tiny Tim's hand-drawn pictures of the family and mail it with insufficient postage.

[1] Unfortunately, this is another instance where cable television has ruined an age of innocence.

[2] Uncharacteristic wisdom and restraint keep me from commenting further here.

[3] I considered commenting on the effect of the USPS "forever stamps." Then I realized that this would require a level of forethought and planning that neither of us has demonstrated.

[4] You will learn more about this in a chapter to come. Do not read ahead. You will spoil the surprise.

VIII

The Fine Line

When I began to establish our nuclear family's tradition of sending a Christmas letter, my spouse had only one concern. She did not want anything in our letter to come across as bragging. I am not sure where she got this streak of Puritan humility, but she was adamant. That eliminated most of the usual topics for a Christmas letter. I could not write about our family vacation if it involved any fun or expense. We could not make anyone feel bad if they were not able to enjoy similar vacation spots. Even the year we drove eight hours to get to the beach where it rained all weekend was off limits. That ruled out ever mentioning trips to Disney World, other countries or even state parks.

Without the ability to write about any of the fun places we went, I was left with little material. The only remaining travels involved visits to relatives' homes. As every child and honest adult will tell you, a trip to visit Aunt and Uncle Whatever is a vacation only in name. You do not have the option of nice rooms at a hotel or beach house. Part of extended family bonding involves everyone sleeping in one building. This is usually a house that now has enough occupants to concern the fire marshal.

The visiting parents get to sleep in the "guest" room. This room contains a mattress that should have gone to the dumpster years ago. The oldest visiting child gets to sleep on the couch that is a mix of French Provincial and Spanish Inquisition. Any remaining children are given sleeping bags for the floor. This floor is covered by what you assume is a carpet and later learn is woven pet hair. This will eventually be determined to be the root cause of your kids' allergies.

Instead of meals at nice restaurants or even fast food establishments, everyone is treated to Aunt Whatever's cooking. Her family can handle the food because they have developed immunities over the years. For the uninitiated visitors, the results are similar to running out of bottled water while in a third world country. On these family visits, there are no trips to the amusement park, miniature golf, or water slides. Instead, everyone is made to watch the poorly edited slideshow from the Whatever family's recent trip to Disney World.

Note that in the Whatever family's rules they are able to both take a fun vacation and talk about it. However nice they may be, they are clearly straying from our shared Puritan roots.

With truly fun vacations removed from the topic list, what remains to fill a page or more of our Christmas letter? This is where your creativity comes into play. To state this clearly, feel free to lie. Why should we hold our Christmas letters to a higher standard than we hold our politicians?

While I would never suggest you tell an obvious lie, there are always opportunities for creative alternatives to the truth.[1] In your Christmas letter, you will find many opportunities to expand on actual events. There is one method I have used to meet my wife's guidelines and yet put our family in a favorable light.

It cannot be considered bragging if it is not true.

Choosing to expand on actual circumstances can save you the embarrassment of being truthful. It can also enhance your social status without the cost of a new wardrobe. Here are just a few examples...

Rather than say that your daughter flunked out of college, say that she is "taking a sabbatical" and "pursuing other interests".

What if your son has a solid D average but continues to play beer pong with the guys in the frat he never was able to join? You can say, "While at the university John found that he was not able to keep up with his academic load and varsity sports. Now he has found an outlet for his competitive spirit by playing in various intramural events."

Instead of saying little Bobby got caught writing bad checks, say he has an appreciation and a talent for doing things "old school."

If Betty has been using a mag stripe reader to

steal credit card numbers then describe her as someone who has a real knack for technology.

If your daughter runs off with the drummer from a Neo-goth/hipster/country-metal band, you can say that she is "pursuing a career in the music industry."

You will find that developing your own creative narratives can add interest to your Christmas letter. As a bonus, these same narratives will also come in handy for your next high school reunion.

Speaking of your class reunion, some people will tell you that living well is the best revenge. If you are not actually living well, then pretending to live well is the next best thing. Let's assume that the senior class voted you "Most Likely to Not" or "Most Likely to Wear a Mullet When He's Forty." You can have sweet revenge by becoming the head of a major corporation in your Christmas letter. Be careful here. You should never name the "major corporation." The list of senior managers at a corporation can be discovered with a single Google search. If you do have to name the corporation for some reason, never claim that you are one of the senior managers. You can simply say that "talks are underway" relative to your new position. While living well might be the best revenge, pretending to live well is the cheapest form of revenge.

It can also be fun to just make up awards and give them to yourself or your immediate family members. Again, if the awards are fictitious then no one can check up on you using Google. The more oblique the reference the better, as in "Our little Johnny was so proud of his award last month. It is rare for someone his age to receive such an honor. He is so humble that he asked that I not include the details in this letter."

If by some remote chance you find it difficult to engage in this level of ~~lying~~ embellishment, I recommend that you spend a few hours watching the political debates from the last election.

"... a lie well told is immortal" - Mark Twain

[1] Obvious lies have consequences. Alternatives to the truth are merely entertaining.

IX

The Internet

The Internet Is God's Way of Saying Plagiarism Is OK

Think back to your school days. Did your teacher ever catch you copying from the encyclopedia[1] for what was to be an original essay? If you were caught borrowing from someone else's creative work then you were punished. This is why you now think it is a bad practice. That lesson may have worked to get you through high school, but now you are an adult and should act like one. As pointed out in the previous chapter, if it is good enough for well-established politicians then it is good enough for you.

You should also gather some comfort from

knowing that no one will be grading your Christmas letter. No one is going to be typing sections of your Christmas letter into Google just to see if you appropriated someone else's intellectual works. Chances are pretty good your Christmas letter, like mine, will never be considered an intellectual work at any level.

You can assume that most of your Christmas letter's reading audience never get past the click-bait titles on Facebook to read an entire online article. The last book they read was assigned in the last class they took, and truth be told they never read that either. So relax and know that if you freely appropriate text from someone else, no one will know unless you are really stupid about it. Since you were smart enough to buy this book I will assume you are not going to be really stupid about it. For those of you who just borrowed this book (and therefore by my consideration are not smart enough to have purchased a copy), I will provide some warnings. If you have any reason to suspect that you are not the brightest star in your family's constellation then be sure to read these warnings.

When your Christmas letter contains

"borrowed" text, follow these guidelines.

1) Never mail a copy to your niece who is an English professor.[2]

2) If you stole/borrowed portions of someone else's Christmas letter then do not mail your letter to that individual or their immediate family. They might catch on if there is a strange congruence between the events described in their last letter and your current letter.

3) When you borrow portions of another Christmas letter, remember to change the names to match your family.

4) When you borrow from any source, be sure to find someone with a similar "voice" to your own. For example, I recently received a Christmas letter that began with the following text.

> "It was the best of times, it was the worst of times, it was the age of wisdom, it was the age of foolishness,..."

It would have worked if they had simply substituted a few words of their own. Here is an example of how to adjust that text to both modernize it and place it in the author's voice.

> "It was the best of times, it was the worst of times, it was the age of wisdom, OMG, it was the age of foolishness, it was the epoch of WTF?..."

5) If you have been whining on Facebook about how your life sucks then do not include any of your Facebook friends on a letter that gushes over with positive news. They may experience a cognitive dissonance.[3]

6) When caught stealing, claim it was meant as a homage and you are so pleased that they noticed the connection.

> "The problem with quotes on the Internet is that it is hard to verify their authenticity."
> ~ Abraham Lincoln[4]

[1] An encyclopedia is a paper version of Wikipedia without Google.

[2] Note that by an English professor I do not mean an individual with a doctorate who also happens to be English. I mean a person who obtained a doctorate in English. Ordinarily, I would not have bothered to point this out, but we established that the people reading this section are potentially not among the Ginsu knives of sharp wits.

[3] Hah! I got you to pull out a dictionary for that one, didn't I?

[4] source: the Internet

X

MOTHER TERESA LETTERS

Not all of us have a nice place in the city and a vacation home in the mountains. We do not all vacation in the locations frequented by the glitterati. I do not even think I would recognize a glitterati if I saw one. Based on the name, I assume one would have to vacuum the couch after their visit. Most of us probably did not trade in our old prop plane for a small jet. In fact, I will wager that few of you have ever had to bother with resurfacing the tennis courts in your backyard.

Unless you are a part of the 1%, you may not be able to share some of these humblebrags in your Christmas letter. This is perfectly understandable and it is really OK. But what do you do if you regularly receive Christmas letters from someone in the top few percent? If you are tired of turning green with envy, you might consider creating a special edition just for those special friends and family. The ones that not only have first-world problems but who have household staff that also only have first-world problems.

Since you cannot compete on an economic level, you can make sure these top-percenters know just how shallow and petty their lives have become. In other words, **if you can't brag about having a better life, make them feel guilty for having one.** This is part of the fine art of humblebragging. This is where you make statements that appear to be self-deprecating or modest but really shine a light on a point of pride.

Here are just a few examples:

> Things are just fine here. I have been disappointed that since catching dengue fever I have not been allowed to return to the mission field. I keep telling Father Thomas that I

am doing much better even though the pain, fever, open sores, and nausea have not subsided as the doctors had predicted.

[Handwritten] *I was sorry to hear that you had a bad cold and hope you recover to full health soon.*

Or,

I hope you are enjoying the Christmas season as I am. I had to stop working from home after we brought three homeless families to live with us. It seemed best to sell my desk so that I could buy a used bunk bed for the twins. Chris has gotten really skilled at stretching our food budget so that what used to feed the two of us can now take care of eighteen hungry mouths.

[Handwritten] *I heard that your patio refrigerator stopped working. Could it be*

*the humidity from the hot tub? In any
case, I hope the manufacturer honors the
warranty.*

Or,

I barely had the energy to complete
my Christmas shopping this year
after all of my visits to the clinic. I
am doing fine on one kidney since I
donated the other one to a neighbor.
I think it may be something else, but
without health insurance, there is no
way of knowing. They do give me a
mini-checkup when I give blood
every other week. Pat tells me I
should not be giving blood at four
different locations. I hate to break
their rules, but I cannot see why I
should not be allowed to offer this
small gift more often than once every
eight weeks. [Handwritten] *I hope
your Shih Tzu does well in therapy. I hate
to think of him struggling with depression*

like that.

Or,

We have racked up a lot of frequent flier miles traveling all over the world. We decided last January that we would go to every active war zone. Once there, we offer ourselves as human shields. It is a small thing, but we feel that if we can keep one innocent from harm then it is worth a little inconvenience for us. We were able to make monthly trips during the first half of the year but have had to cut back as our recovery time has gone up along with the number of our wounds. Or perhaps it is just a side benefit of getting older? LOL. [Handwritten] *Tough luck losing the handicap sticker on your Benz. I don't think government officials understand the agony of tennis elbow. Get better soon.*

You get the idea.[1]

It won't make up for the fact that you do not have a vacation home, but it may make their Christmas Eve lobster bisque a bit less tasty.

A side benefit can be found if you give the one-percent crowd a link to donate to your personal "charity." As long as you do not claim to be a 501(c)3 non-profit, what is the harm? You get a few dollars through PayPal and they get to soothe their conscience. Sounds like a win-win to me. However, this only works with friends and family who live some distance from you and do not talk to your other friends and family members. Observing this caution can save embarrassment and a pesky refund process.

[1] At least I hope you do by now. There are limits to what even an accomplished teacher can do.

XI

I Was Joking You

As we have seen in the last chapters, veracity is highly overrated. However, I would be doing you a disservice if I were to imply that there was no risk involved.

Your embellishments can become problematic if you get too specific. For example, never say you were elected to the office of President of the United States of America. A clever someone might be able to check the records and find out this was not true. Let us assume the highest office you have ever held was that of board member at your mobile home park. You would be better to write something like, "I have been considering saying, 'yes' to my party's call to run for office." You do not need to tell them which party or what office. You need never actually obtain an office to get credit for just being considered.

If all else fails and you are caught in an obvious fabrication, you can fall back on the line one of my daughters would frequently use as a toddler. When caught in an obvious lie she would simply smile and say, "I was joking you!" It rarely worked for her, but you might give it a try.

XII

They Are Lying Too

There is a chance that you feel inadequate knowing that you are ~~lying~~ enhancing the truth in your Christmas letter. You should gain some comfort in knowing that the Christmas letters you receive are full of just as many fabrications. Look at the names from your Christmas card list. You have known most of these people for years. You know them and their progeny and what they're capable of. No matter what their past letters may have claimed, you know in your heart that their life is probably no better than yours.

Remember that the definition of a dysfunctional family is "a family with more than one member." Each family just provides their own unique spin on dysfunction. Some are simply more talented in spinning than others.

Keep this in mind when you receive a happy-happy Christmas letter from a friend. I assure you that their son's "internship with a recording company" really means that he is a roadie for a Guns N' Roses cover band.

XIII

REFERENCE WORKS

We live in a time of computer-based writing
tools and Internet reference sites. With these
advantages, you may think there is simply no
reason for not using concise and precise
language in your Christmas letter. After all, the
main purpose of using plain words and simple,
direct sentences is to clearly communicate. Do I
need to remind you that clear communication is
not one of the goals of a Christmas letter? This
is why I am the **accomplished teacher** and
you are the student.

I would hope that by now you would
understand why you should use a thesaurus.
Using big words in your writing will make you
appear smarter than your audience. Keep in
mind that it is is easier to ~~fool~~ persuade an

impressed reader. Or said another way, "Utilizing sesquipedalian locution in your epistle will insinuate that you are more perspicacious than your coterie, and an individual with a predilection is easier to beguile." Big words will help you obfuscate the details that you wish to obfuscate. Isn't that obvious?

Along with a thesaurus, you might find a dictionary comes in handy in some situations. If you are concerned that you may be caught in an embellishment, a dictionary can help you out. Use the dictionary to find a positive word that is similar to the more accurate negative word. This lets you use a variation on the "blasted autocorrect" excuse.

As an example, you might be concerned that your daughter's work in a beauty shop is not going to engender the right degree of envy in your readers. Still, you hesitate to push things too far. You can comfortably write in your Christmas letter that your daughter is studying cosmology. If one of your readers happens to see her working at Sally Sue's Beauty Emporium, you can easily blame the autocorrect. The shared hatred we all have towards rogue autocorrect software will create a strong bond between you and your reader.

XIV

Your Voice

It is essential that you write your Christmas letter using your own voice.

Using your own voice sounds simple, but what if your voice is tinny, too nasal, screechy or whiny? Did you forget that a Christmas letter is a written communication? Your reader is reading and not listening. The timbre of your voice will not be a problem. You only need to worry about the tone that you convey through your words. You are on the way to solving that problem as you work your way through this book.

Even if you are not concerned about your vocal cords, you might think this year it is time to do something different. You may want to see if it is possible to make this year's Christmas letter fresh, clever and entertaining. One approach would be to use the voice of some other individual or even the voice of another species.

We need to face some hard facts here. You are not the author of *Watership Down*. You may have watched *Look Who's Talking* a dozen times, but it does not give you the delivery of Bruce Willis.[1]

You may think that writing from the perspective of your newborn will be humorous. It will be. But only to you.

Most writers consider their written works to be their children. This is a valuable metaphor for this discussion. In particular, I want you to think of your child's-voice Christmas letter as your baby. No matter how much you love this particular baby, this baby is ugly. I realize it would help to have another metaphor here. I seriously searched for a better metaphor. With or without a better metaphor, don't use a child's voice for your letter.

There is a familiar mechanism at work here. One of the secrets behind the survival of our species is that parents think their own children are good-looking from the moment they come out of the womb as misshapen lumps. This notion persists through the terrible twos and on up to whatever age they are now. You think your young ones are completely adorable. Unfortunately, you are missing the fact that children like yours are the cause of our country's declining birth-rate.

Young couples may tell you that they are "just not ready for kids." The truth is they are afraid, very afraid, of producing one or more children that may turn out like yours. A well-kept secret is that the divorce rate in this country is being held artificially low. Millions of couples would divorce today if they could agree on which one of them has to take the children.

Keep this in mind before you subject your friends and family to a Christmas letter written from the perspective of a small child. Children are adorable when they speak a single cute phrase. That lasts until the third sentence. From there it gets tedious.

There are similar reasons to avoid writing your Christmas letter using the "voice" of your pet or any animal. Many people before you have written these chronically un-cute Christmas letters. If God had wanted the family cat or dog to write letters, he would have given them opposable thumbs. He chose not to and who are we to question the Almighty?

Even more disturbing, I have read Christmas letters written as if the author was a squirrel inhabiting a tree in the backyard. Why someone would want to portray a squirrel as some variety of Peeping Tom or stalker is beyond me. The poor rodent's life is difficult enough without this added burden. They already have to deal with the effects of global warming and the neighbor kid's new pellet gun.

Here is the simple rule: Never write a Christmas letter in the voice of an animal. It just embarrasses you and demeans the animal, except in the cases where it demeans you and embarrasses the animal.

Either way, it is not a good idea for your letter. You also need to be concerned if a copy of that letter ever falls into the hands of a rabid PETA member. From what I understand, they are not a group that appreciates humor or understands forgiveness.[2]

For similar reasons, do not use your letter to give voice to inanimate objects. It may sound interesting at first, but it quickly becomes Stephen King-ish or M. Night Shyamalan-esque. I am already afraid of the Elf on the Shelf and suspect SIRI knows more about me than she lets on.

Once you apply all of the wisdom I share in this book I guarantee that you will write a wonderful, witty, and entertaining Christmas letter. Unless you don't and then I do not guarantee a thing.

In any event, make your mistakes in your own voice and leave small children, animals, and your readers in peace.

[1] If you do attempt to use the voice of Bruce Willis, make sure you rented *Look Who's Talking* and not *Die Hard*.
[2] Note to any rabid PETA members: I was joking you. Please forgive me.

XV

1 Picture = 1000 Words

A Picture Is Worth 1000 Words But Uses a Lot More Ink.

Just as I must assume few readers will have made it to this point, you should assume that most of your "readers" are really "skimmers". Some may not even skim the text but just glance at the pictures. To accomplish your goal of producing a certain level of envy in the skimmers and glancers, you should focus on getting the right pictures to include in your letter.

There is an art to making you and your family look better than you really are. One of the easiest methods is to avoid showing a picture of your actual family. Instead, find a picture of a group that is more attractive and have better haircuts. If your immediate family is not that good-looking (be honest here, they aren't), then you need to find suitable replacements.

As with most tasks today, you go first to the Internet. After wasting forty minutes on Facebook, you begin by searching any one of the stock photo websites. Be sure that you are visiting a reputable website. Avoid any with taglines such as "people of Walmart," "ugly matching sweaters," and "awkward family photos." If you are visiting one of those sites please do not be shocked. You may see a picture of your family from last year's Christmas letter. This is just one of the many reasons you needed to purchase this book.

If you are not Internet literate, simply go to your local department store and shop in the aisle with photo frames. Most of these frames come with a photo of an average family. This family is average if your idea of average includes good teeth, great hair, and clothing from a better store than you are in at the moment. Unlike your family, the people in this manufactured family are all smiling and have their eyes open in spite of the flash. They are also good-looking. They are always really good-looking to the point where it may seem unnatural. For the price of a cheap frame, you have a picture of your new and improved substitute family. Your Christmas letter recipients should find themselves looking at this group of impossibly attractive people and wondering which one is you.

I do have a few warnings that you should heed if you choose a picture perfect family from a frame or stock photo site.

- Pick a family that matches your real family in number and distribution. This will remove the requirement for one or more explanatory paragraphs in your letter.
- Diversity is a wonderful thing and our country is blessed to be the home of people from many parts of the world. That said, this may not be the best time to drastically change your family's ancestral heritage. If you do, I would love to hear how you explain this in your letter.
- If you scan a previously-framed picture, remember to use a photo editor to erase

the barcode and price tag in the lower right corner. Your audience may be bright enough to see through your attempt to deceive.

Whether you find the picture of your desired family on the Internet or in the frame aisle at Target,[1] look for a picture where everyone is wearing clothing from the same color palette. You might think they are just being conformist, but what this really demonstrates is this family has money to burn. Most families take pictures with everyone wearing their "church clothes." The picture frame family can afford to buy an additional set of clothing to ensure they will all match for the picture. All white sweaters, shirts, pants, and shorts on an ocean beach seem to be a favorite for some reason. In any case, this family grouping will never again be seen together in these clothes. What looks really "put together" in a family photo looks like a cult when you see them on the street.

One problem with using a scanned or a stock family photo is that the people in them never age. You should not use the same picture year after year. Eventually, someone will notice that the kids do not get any taller and the parents do not get any grayer, shorter, wrinkled, etc. On the other hand, many of your readers think *The Curious Case of Benjamin Button* was based on a true story.

I am sure that there are a few of you that are comfortable with the written fabrications described in previous chapters. Yet you still insist on using actual pictures of your real family. This may be a result of some lingering sense of honesty. It may be a mistaken belief that you and your kids actually look good in your last group picture. You know, the one where you were all together at your nephew's wedding and it was after the wine toast but before the jello shots. Or possibly you still love the cute picture where everyone in the family had matching pajamas or Halloween costumes. If this is the case, do another Internet search for "awkward family photos" and see if you are there.

I am sure there are at least of few who remain unconvinced. If you still want to use actual family pictures, my advice is that you let your teenager Photoshop the crap out of them. Depending on their skills, this may be challenging but remember:

God would not have allowed
Photoshop to exist if he didn't want
us to appear better than we really
are.

[1] I do not recommend you get your photo frames at one of the everything-for-a-dollar stores. As in many things, you get what you pay for. Your family deserves to pretend to be the people in a Target frame - or better.

XVI

Reboot as Needed

At this point, you may be saying to yourself, "I have dug myself into a deep hole with five or ten years of Christmas letters that were boring and/or too honest. Why didn't I find this wonderful, cheap-at-any-price book several years ago?"

I hate to interrupt you when you are having a conversation with yourself, but I have some good news for you. It is not too late. You can start again. Tomorrow is the first day of the rest of your life.[1] You can reboot your life starting with this year's Christmas letter.

If you have not noticed, reboots are all the rage. There was a reboot of Star Trek and there are few cows more sacred. Each generation seems to have their own movie version of Batman and Spiderman. Thanks to our short attention spans, some generations have more than one. If it works for Hollywood, it can work for you.

There is no reason that you can't do a reboot of your life. This is particularly true if your audience is primarily American. Many articles, that I honestly intended to read, have documented our reduced attention span and declining long-term memory. If this wasn't true, our political system would never work for more than one cycle. As Americans, we can be distracted by something shiny dangling in front of us. If it makes a liberal amount of noise, even better. Unless you vote red and then it should make a conservative amount of noise.[2] Do not be concerned that your readers might spot discrepancies between this year's Christmas letter and one from a previous year. Odds are they will not remember the content even if they did read past the second paragraph.

The reboot process can be very liberating. You can start today. Make yourself into a new person without the effort of working out, attending night school, taking lessons in etiquette, or any other form of masochism masquerading as self-improvement. You can create a new family in the image of the family you always wanted and deserve. Even better, you can do this without going through the children's difficult years.[3] You just need to start writing Christmas letters from this point forward using the wisdom of this book.

Remember, few people have read all of your previous letters. They may have glanced at the pictures but will not recall which ones were your family or some other family. Also, in past years you were producing Christmas letters that were so ordinary no reader could tell which letter in the stack came from which family. The reboot promises no risk and very high rewards. Just stay away from a reboot of the Incredible Hulk or Godzilla. Those never work out.

[1] Unfortunately, this also means that today is the last day of the start of your life.

[2] This is the third time I've used a variation on this joke. Repeating a joke twice is bad writing. Using a joke three times makes it a running joke. Four or more times and it becomes your trademark.

[3] The children's "difficult years" are the years between birth and their first real job.

XVII

SOME EXAMPLES

If you are like me, you are basically lazy.[1] That means that even with the help of this book, you might not gather the energy or take the time to write a decent Christmas letter. This chapter and the next will save the day. In this chapter, I will provide some actual, names-have-been-changed-to-protect-the-innocent examples of situations that may apply to your family. Then I will show what you can do with each seemingly hopeless case to put a positive spin on it.

Our first example involves a friend's daughter who has had an unfortunate disagreement with law enforcement. As a result, she finds herself incarcerated. Unless this is a point of pride with your family (which it might be - I'm not judging here), you may want to come up with a more creative description.

The following is an excerpt from a friend's recent Christmas letter.

> We were saddened this year to learn that Jenny's appeal had been turned down. She was picked up on Main Street last week along with the friends she calls her "posse." I thought the posse was supposed to be the good guys. Anyway, she is now serving a 5-to-10 sentence in the state prison up the road. On the bright side, we have all begun to learn some new vocabulary as a result of her prison experiences.

Wrong. Wrong. Wrong. First of all, no one wants to hear that you were saddened by anything. This is the Christmas season after all. Our own dysfunctional families and mounting credit card bills are enough to depress us. Why would we want to hear about anything that saddens you? Second, while this paragraph may be factual, is it really what you want to communicate with the judgmental people in your hometown? Try this paragraph instead.

We were glad this year to hear that Jenny had a great new opportunity. As of last week, she has a full-time position with the state. All of her benefits, including accommodations, are part of the deal. She was not expecting it. In fact, they literally "grabbed her off the street" along with a number of her work associates. Several senior government officials were eager to see her. They were insistent and made her an offer that she could not refuse. She has been guaranteed a position for at least five and possibly ten years. On the downside, her new role does not provide any opportunities for travel. However, in this economy, she is very fortunate to have this degree of stability.

Isn't that better? This version meets all of our criteria. It is upbeat (we were glad this year). It is factual (five to ten years with no chance of travel). It will make people envious of you (Jenny is in demand). Building on this success let's try another.

May-December Romance - Before

> We are not sure why, but our little Madge left home early in the year and we have not seen her since. It started when she began dating a 58-year-old ex-con who sports several colorful, self-inflicted tattoos. We know him only as "Snake." The last we saw of Madge, she was riding away on the back of his motorcycle headed to God knows where.

May-December Romance - After

> We are thrilled that there is a new

man in Madge's life. He is an accomplished traveler and an artist with a style of his own. We are hoping that his interest in Ophiology will rekindle her interest in the sciences. While there are no definite plans for a wedding at this point, they are doing some traveling together. One never knows where that will lead.

Academics - Before

We have no idea what Brenda is going to do now that she has been kicked out of every junior college in the state. We were hoping that her juvenile record would not follow her. It turns out it is not as difficult to get court proceedings unsealed as you would think.

Academics - After

We are so proud of Brenda and her focus on learning rather than simply gathering degrees. Several academic institutions have been reviewing her records and she is considering her options.

Career in Sports - Before

John was not able to land a spot on the professional video game team as he had hoped. He did not even get a call for tryouts after the team manager told him he was suffering from "a complete lack of talent." Now he just sits in the basement, looking at his Pokémon cards and searching for more on eBay. He needs money to live on, so he is selling off his duplicates. Even for the best ones, he is lucky to get a dollar. When he is not on eBay, he is on Facebook. We argue about it all the time now. This life seems to make sense to him, but I just don't get it.

Career in Sports - After

Jonathan has achieved his goal of finding his passion and his life's work in the same place. After a medical situation forced him to give up his dream of playing video games professionally, he searched for and found his perfect vocation. He has tried to explain it to me several times. My layman's understanding is that he has formed a small internet trading company. Utilizing social media, he is able to market select items of collectible memorabilia to people around the country.

Financial Situation - Before

Tom has had a string of bad luck lately. We thought we had everything handled after the whole fraudulent check thing blew over. Then we learned of the massive credit card charges he had piled up from in-game purchases on "Candy Crush Saga." It seems that bankruptcy is the only option for Tom at this point, as he has nothing left for them to take. As far as our situation, we hope the court will let us hold on to the house in spite of the fact that Tom listed it as an asset on several of his bad loans.

Financial Situation - After

Thomas has recently achieved a new level of happiness. After pursuing a traditional lifestyle focused on accumulation, he has decided to divest himself of earthly possessions for the purity of a simple life. We really envy his ability to focus on this almost spiritual approach to possessions. We are learning from him every day. Who knows? Perhaps one day we will follow his example.

Extreme Examples - Before

Your child decides to become an artist, musician,[2] professional fantasy sports competitor or run for elected office.

Extreme Examples - After

There is nothing to say here. You might want to quietly drop this child from your family. An alternative is to only include page one of a letter that appears to continue on to a second page. Of course, there is no second page. That lets you avoid any topics that are impossible to gloss over or describe creatively.

[1] I actually do not consider myself lazy. I prefer to think that I am able to focus on

finding the most efficient means to tackle a particular task. This focus may require some time to produce results. That may mean I complete my search for efficiencies long after the need for the task is past. I cannot be held accountable for the world choosing to label my genius as "lazy."

[2] Or even worse, a drummer.

XVIII

DIY Letter

If you do not have the time or the ability to write your own letter, I have provided a short but complete example here. You can simply enter this letter into your word processor, change the names, and add a few personal touches to make it your own. Each sentence of mine is intended to give you a kernel to expand into a paragraph or more. Do not get too carried away with personalization however because we have already agreed at the start of this paragraph that you may lack the necessary ability.

Dear Loved Ones,

This year has been filled with many

delights for our household as well as some challenges. I will begin by sharing what is happening in the kids' lives. We have enjoyed watching Buffy and Jody move from one accomplishment to the next. As you would expect, they are typical teenagers with all of the joys that come from being that age.

After the wonderful times we had this last summer, Chris and I remarked on how much we both loved the Caribbean. The flight is so much shorter than the one to Hawaii. We also think the Caribbean provides more fun for each dollar spent.

What can I say about work? I have been able to explore the workings of other groups through a cross-functional opportunity. As a result, I have new responsibilities at work and that has been taking more of my time. I guess that is why they call it work. LOL.

As for hobbies, Chris and I have enjoyed spending more time in the yard this year. There is something special in watching what you planted come to life. We have gone so far as to offer our services to several of our neighbors. Not everyone has the time or physical ability that we do. We are happy that we can serve others in this small way and they seem to appreciate it.

Best wishes from our family.

Signed by all

To help you understand how to use this letter, I will break it down piece by piece so that you can see how it works.

Dear Loved Ones,

It does not hurt to stroke their ego by referring to them as "Loved Ones". It is particularly valuable when you send this to the people that cannot stand you. It will start them off feeling guilty and a little unworthy themselves. This is right where you want them.

This year has been filled with many delights for our household as well as some challenges.

Specific words are important here. The use of "delights" will tantalize them. They personally have not experienced anything they would consider a delight in the past year. The creation of envy starts here. Using "household" rather than the more pedestrian "family" or "house" gives you an air of "Downton Abby" without the salary requirements of servants. The reference to "challenges" is also important. It tells the reader that while you have faced adversity, in the end, you triumphed. Again, this develops envy in the reader. By comparison, their life was filled with numerous mundane annoyances and nothing worthy of being labeled as a challenge.

I will begin by sharing what is happening in the kids' lives.

This is a good place to start, but you should expect to lose half of your audience right here.

We have enjoyed watching Buffy and Jody move from one accomplishment to the next.

Obviously, you should replace "Buffy and Jody" with the names of your own children unless you were really that big a fan of "Family Affair."[1] The beauty of this sentence is that you do not have to be specific regarding the accomplishments. It could be that after several attempts your children finally made it out of sixth grade. Not knowing this, your reader will assume they have been given early admission to an Ivy League school with both athletic and scholastic scholarships.

As you would expect, they are typical teenagers with all of the

joys that come from being that age.
Once again, your readers will fill in the blanks
with images of *the Brady Bunch* while you were
really thinking *Children of the Corn.*

**After the wonderful times we had
this last summer, Chris and I
remarked on how much we both
loved the Caribbean. The flight is
so much shorter than the one to
Hawaii. We also think the
Caribbean provides more fun for
each dollar spent.**
This paragraph is an excellent example of
literary slight of hand. The reader will be left
with two positive impressions. The first is that
you and your spouse were able to have a
wonderful vacation in the Caribbean. The
second is that while you enjoyed the delights of
the food, drink, sun-filled days and music-filled
nights, you were still being responsible with your
money. While this paragraph will leave those
impressions, it does not actually claim that you
went to the Caribbean. Your "wonderful times"
could well have been drinking lukewarm
domestic beer in your backyard. All you are

saying is that you and your spouse talked about how much you loved the Caribbean. You never admit that your love for the island life has never been consummated.

What can I say about work? I have been able to explore the workings of other groups through a cross-functional opportunity.
Spending days being questioned by the Human Resources representative does give you a certain appreciation for their department.

As a result, I have new responsibilities at work and that has been taking more of my time.
Once again, you cannot be held responsible for the assumptions made by others. Readers may understandably jump to the conclusion that you received a big promotion. There is no reason to fill in the details of the suspected but unproven, embezzlement and your demotion from management to the stockroom.

I guess that is why they call it work. LOL.

When you need filler, you can always fall back on a cliché backed up with a worn-out pop culture reference.

As for hobbies, Chris and I have enjoyed spending more time in the yard this year. There is something special in watching what you planted come to life. We have gone so far as to offer our services to several of our neighbors.

You should be able to work this one out on your own by now. Money has been tight since your demotion. You have started mowing lawns in the neighborhood to make ends meet.

Not everyone has the time or physical ability that we do. We are happy that we can serve others in this small way -

Turn the source of embarrassment into an opportunity to shame others. The implication is that you are mowing the lawn of the senior citizens next door.

- and they seem to appreciate it.

Even in lawn maintenance, tips are welcomed.

Best wishes from our family.

This should come from your heart or if that doesn't work, do a Google search for "sincere Christmas wish".

Signed by all[2]

If you make no other changes to the letter, you must delete this and insert your actual name(s). I asked several friends to test this letter last year. The one who left this signature line intact was not seen as genuine by their recipients.

If this still seems like too much work for you, I am offering my letter-writing services to a select few. Contact me directly and I am sure we can work out a price that I will consider fair.

---

[1] If you went so far as to name a pet "Mr. French" then put this book down and seek help immediately.

[2] If your family are all hardcore *Battlestar Galactica* fans, "Signed by all" may be replaced by "So Say We All!"

XIX

DON'TS

I tried to be positive. I really did. But I would not be doing my duty to you (or my word count) if I did not include an additional list of things to avoid in your Christmas letter. There are bits of advice scattered across each chapter, but here is a list of additional things to avoid.

1) Stay far away from certain taboo topics such as politics, your catheter, or bowel obstructions. I would not think it would be necessary to list these but based on a few letters I received last year, apparently it is. If you wonder why I list politics with the other two, you obviously have not been paying attention to the news.

2) Do not write poetry. Count the number of subscriptions you have to poetry magazines.

Why is that? Because no one reads poetry outside of English class and the occasional hipster cafe doing a retro-beatnik event. The only possible exception would be a letter composed as a limerick. Bear in mind that the only limericks that are funny are risqué. Look carefully at your expected audience before you try this.

3) Do not list the family members you visited over the summer. The family you visited already know that you were there. Everyone else doesn't care.

4) Do not ridicule any group that sets off car bombs. These individuals do not have a sense of humor. Remember that your Christmas letter comes in an envelope with your return address.

5) Do not make fun of white supremacists. Yes, they deserve it. Yes, they are easy prey. Once again, they do not have a sense of humor. They also have a highly tuned and well-deserved persecution complex.

6) Do not write poetry. I realize this is a repeat, but I am worried that some of you may not have gotten the point the first time. You will

note that there are no rhyme schemes in this entire book. It is better for it.

XX

No Card for You

To remain in polite society, you have two options. If you choose not to write a Christmas letter then your alternative is a Christmas card. It sounds like it would be a simpler solution, but there are pitfalls. Ask yourself if you want to be judged solely on the quality of the card you choose.

To begin with, consider the places you normally shop. I will guess the store's name includes "dollar" or ends in "mart". Buy your Christmas cards there and everyone will know what a cheap bastard you really are. However, if you move to an upscale store, your expensive card will not fool anyone. You should not even try that approach. These are your friends and family members after all. They have seen you sneak your own candy and pop into movie theaters since you were seven. They will see your expensive card for what it is - a low-effort, out of character, effort to buy their admiration.

At this point, you are telling yourself that if cheap and expensive cards are both out then you will get something that falls in between. Nice try. The card manufacturers are on to you and your attempts to take the Mama Bear way out. They do not offer anything in between. Shop around and you will find that if the card looks nice, you cannot afford to buy one for everyone on your list. If you can afford it, it looks like it was printed in a factory that once built Yugos.

This is a no-win situation so you may as well get back on the Christmas letter bandwagon. That is why you picked up this book after all.

XXI

IN CLOSING

Close Like You Mean It

If you are keeping track of the page number or the Kindle percentage read, you have no doubt guessed that you are nearing the end of our little adventure. Before we move from the chapters you only skimmed to the appendices you will ignore, we need to talk about how to close your Christmas letter.

In spite of the occasional less-than-serious remarks I've made about the art of Christmas letters, we need to remember that Christmas is a special season. Your letter should end with a solemn reminder of this and a wish for peace on earth. If you do this well, you will make it clear to all that you are a Truly Good Person. Not only that, but you are a much better person than those who caved and sent generic "Happy Holidays" cards. The difficulty is to make this believable. If you can accomplish this you are an artist and possibly have a career ahead of you in marketing.

Moving from general to specific ...

I have often said that a writer should plagiarize the best and when you cannot do that, then plagiarize yourself. With that as justification, I am including excerpts from some of the Christmas letters I have written over the years. Specifically, I am using excerpts from the closings since I noticed that is part of this chapter's title. Use these examples to spark your own creative closing.

1997 - As we look back on this last year, we remember the wonderful times we had with family and friends and count our many blessings. We pray that you are feeling the joy of the Christmas Season. If your house is like ours, peace may be too much to hope for.

2005 - To those of you that have not seen us in recent years, we miss you and hope to see you soon. To those of you that have seen us recently, I apologize. We'll behave better next time. I promise.

2006 - I could go on some more about my wonderful wife and kids, but I can sense that you are starting to yawn. If you still have the letter opener in your hand, put it down before you hurt yourself.

2009 - As always, we are thankful for our many blessings - our family, our friends, our home and free shipping from Amazon.com. We wish all the best for you in the coming year.

"Sincerity is the most important thing. If you can fake that, you've got it made." - Unknown source

XXII

Insert Your Holiday

I could not complete this book without including a chapter describing how these methods apply to other varieties of holiday letters, specifically Hanukkah letters, Kwanza letters, and others. While my personal practice is to send a Christmas letter, I realize there are many people of other faiths and beliefs. I would not want to leave these readers with no idea how to write their letters. More to the point, I would not want to miss the potential sales. Therefore at the risk of offending any groups that I have not offended in the previous chapters, here goes.

Hanukkah - I will admit to not having much knowledge when it comes to Hanukkah. I grew up in South Dakota where our understanding of diversity was somewhat limited by our lack of diversity. I do know that family Hanukkah celebrations owe a great deal to Christmas celebrations. Jewish children would not receive as many presents if their parents weren't conscious of the need to one-up Santa Claus.

Kwanzaa - By including Kwanzaa on the list I have probably convinced some readers that I am just being politically correct. Others will accuse me of cultural appropriation. To both groups, I would just point out that thanks to Wikipedia, at least I spelled it correctly.

Winter solstice - I included this for completeness, but let's be honest with each other. Did you really think I was going to say anything meaningful? The other holidays have either special foods, parties, presents or all of the above. What does winter solstice have? The only people that really celebrate it get half their year's income during the four weekends the Renaissance Fair is open. That does not leave a lot left over for a December celebration other than dancing naked in the woods with leaves in your hair.

To make effective use of this book within other cultures and religious traditions, simply make use of one of the following transpositions as appropriate.

1) Every time you see the word "Christmas" pronounce it as "Ha nuk kah".
Or
2) Every time you see the word "Christmas" pronounce it as "Kwan zaa".
Or
3) Every time you see the word "Christmas" say something in the Druid language. Use Klingon as a substitute if you do not know any Druid. Most people who know one will be familiar with the other.

XXIII

Penultimate Chapter

I do not have any content for this chapter, but I really liked the title. Given that title, there was only one place to put it.

There is good news if you are one of those compulsive people who have to finish every book you start. You are almost there. If this was a novel, you would be holding your breath. The climax would occur right about … wait for it … let the suspense build … now.

Since this is not a novel, you may now let out your breath.

XXIV

PUTTING IT ALL TOGETHER

In conclusion, …

Do not take it too seriously. Have fun.

Write something you would enjoy reading.

If you do not have much to say, use a bigger font.

Tell a story. Facts and dates are boring. Stories entertain.

Write simple sentences.[1]

Don't fret over it. You will get another chance next year.

[1] This helps you avoid any need for semicolons.

Why Trust Me?

If you jumped to this part of the book, I will assume it is because you were directed here from the "Your Audience" chapter. In that case, skip the following paragraph.

If you got here by browsing the Table of Contents, then I am concerned. What was it in the title that brought you here? I suspect this goes past a healthy level of skepticism and shows that you have real trust issues. Your problems go beyond any that can be addressed by a Christmas letter, no matter how good it may be. You may want to see someone about this before continuing with the rest of this book.

For the rest of you, the ones without trust issues, we can continue. I can answer the "why trust me?" question with a simple response. I am the author of this book. You should have been trained from a young age to trust authors. The alternative is to spend a great deal of time as your own fact checker. If that is necessary then you got to this paragraph under false pretenses and need to go back to the previous paragraph.[1]

If anyone is still with me, I hope the "I am the author" argument was sufficient. There is also the agreement we made in the Preface that I was to be your **accomplished teacher**. I am willing to play fast and loose with the facts in a Christmas letter. However, as the author and as your Christmas letter mentor, I would never do anything to cause you to lose faith in me. Unless I thought I could get away with it.

With that settled, you should go back to wherever you were when you jumped to this chapter.

[1] I did not intend that this book become a make-your-own-adventure, but you are driving me in that direction.

A Retrospective

In preparing this book, I learned a great many interesting facts. Only a few were related to the topic at hand. That seems to be what happens when you give someone with ADD access to Wikipedia. For example, I learned that Christmas letters are called "round robin letters" in the United Kingdom. The origins of this name are shrouded in a touch of mystery and a great deal of apathy. From what I can tell, this is just another example of the whimsical word choice of the British. I firmly believe that they agreed to call a wrench a spanner after a late night at the pub. Anyone can tell that a wrench is a wrench just by looking at it.

Leaving British word choice aside, I was able to learn a few on-topic facts as I bounced between and across hyperlinks. It turns out that the first Christmas card was created in 1843. This new invention was in response to the proliferation of Christmas letters. Sir Henry Cole had "too many friends." He did not have time to pen a letter in response to every Christmas letter he received. The Christmas card was created to be a less labor-intensive option. Since Sir Henry created his impersonal-but-efficient Christmas card in 1843, we can assume Christmas letters existed sometime before that year.

I honestly made an effort to do more research on the history of Christmas letters. Unfortunately, the only thing more boring than most Christmas letters is researching the history of Christmas letters.

ACKNOWLEDGMENTS

In the book you just read, you learned that few people enjoy reading your annual Christmas letter. The same can be said of the acknowledgments section of any book. The fact that you are reading this section has one of several possible causes.

First of all, you could be an extremely polite individual. Extremely polite people are willing to read acknowledgments because they feel it would be rude not to do so. The author put time and effort into writing the acknowledgments. Out of respect for the author, the acknowledgments deserve to be read. That is very sweet of you but could be a byproduct of your crippling insecurities.

If you are not that polite, you might be reading this section out of compulsion. You could be blessed with a level of disorder that requires you to finish every page once you begin reading anything. This might explain why you have two closets overflowing with back issues of *Time* magazine. I am sure you will get around to them soon.

Finally, you may know or suspect that you are one of the lucky few whose contributions are noted by the author. You want to check to see if your name is here and what praise you may have received. That makes you more than just a bit narcissistic, don't you think?

The conclusion we have to reach is that anyone reading this far is dealing with one or more potentially serious psychological conditions. While this book can help you write a Christmas letter that doesn't suck, it will not help you deal with your larger issues.

All is not lost. Do not despair even if you are also prone to that. This book will help you write a humorous and readable Christmas letter. With that letter, you will be able to convince your friends and family that you have gotten past all of your potentially serious psychological conditions. After accomplishing that, you can get the professional help you desperately need. Then you will no longer feel you must read these acknowledgments.

However, you are currently still insecure, compulsive, or narcissistic. Possibly all of the above. It is for you that I write the remainder of this acknowledgments section.

This book would not exist without the encouragement of many friends and family members. I want to sincerely, and I do mean sincerely, thank everyone who provided me with comments on my Christmas letters.[1]

I need to make special mention of Jim Schrempp, Phil Grant, and Carl Wysocki. These three provided valuable feedback and this book is better for their efforts. If that makes you wonder what it was like in earlier versions, then you understand why you should also thank them. It takes a good friend to be willing to provide direct, constructive, and, at times, harsh comments. These three are such good friends that they were not only willing to make harsh comments but seemed to enjoy it.

Though too numerous to list individually, I want to thank the members the Atlanta Writers Club. In particular, the talented individuals of my critique group let me learn from their example each week. In hindsight, I should have joined this group years before. They might have been able to stop me.

Most of all, I want to thank my lovely wife and my beautiful children for their love and support. This time I do mean it. Really. I mostly meant it on the dedications page, but I completely mean it now.

I would be remiss at this point if I did not offer at least a few apologies as well. My first apology is to all of you dear readers. I used "remiss" in the first sentence of this paragraph in an effort to deceive. While I took the required freshman English class, it was not my finest hour. I filled the next three years of my schedule with math, computer science, and philosophy courses. Had I known I would later write a book, I would have taken a few more English courses.

That said, the freshman English course is where I learned that the rules of good writing could be bent or even broken. If we are expected to forgive Hemingway for being terse and Faulkner for writing run-on sentences, then you can cut me some slack. While they may have produced some classic works in the past, neither one has produced anything of note in over thirty years. I, on the other hand, have not produced anything of note far more recently.

My next apology is to everyone who feels that I may have poked gentle fun at the Christmas letters they sent to me over the years. In point of fact, I am not poking gentle fun at these letters; I border on being nasty. It may seem at times like I am stabbing you in the heart. I apologize for anything in this book that seems to insult anyone other than myself. In general, I try to stick to self-deprecating humor. I have found I am the person least likely to sue me. Unfortunately, it is difficult to write a book when I am the target of every punch line. This is the only reason that I have included a few jabs at others. I hope you understand I am laughing with you and not at you. You are laughing, aren't you?

Finally, if I have missed anyone who feels they deserve an apology, I apologize. You obviously were not important enough for me to even remember how I had wronged you. That or I felt the perceived hurt was not great enough to deserve an apology. On the other hand, it may be that I just missed it altogether. In any case, I suggest we both get over it. If you will, I will.

[1] While most of those on our mailing list have been gracious, I have a special message for the people who return the unopened envelopes marked "return to sender." The post office uses a stamp for this. Your handwritten version is not fooling anyone.

BIBLIOGRAPHY

Dickens, Charles (1843) A Christmas Carol

Dickens, Charles (1859) A Tale of Two Cities

ITunes Store: Music, search = "the 12 days of Christmas"; 2017

Citations: Speeding, Violation of noise control ordinance (vehicle), failure to yield to school bus

About the Author

Chuck Storla began his writing career at an early age. He started with block letters and after mastering both upper and lowercase moved on to cursive. In addition to writing, he has been an avid reader of chapter books for much of his adult life.

After graduating from college, he ignored his muse and followed a paycheck. This led to a successful career in technology and introduced him to the joys of middle management. Upon leaving the corporate world, he rediscovered his inner artist. As of this printing, his works have been printed in dozens of fonts all over the world. This assumes your view of the world is limited to the countries eligible to compete in the World Series.

You can learn more about the fascinating world of Chuck Storla at the eponymous website - chuckstorla.com. He wanted to get in the word "eponymous" somewhere and this was the last opportunity.

THANK YOU

Thank you for taking time to read *Zen and the Art of Christmas Letters*. If you enjoyed it, please consider telling your friends or posting a short review. I appreciate your kind words.

If you did not enjoy it, let's keep that between us. You already have a reputation as a negative person. There is no need to cement that impression.

Made in the USA
Columbia, SC
07 November 2021